GET TO
KNOW CLASSICAL
MASTERPIECES

T0085662

George Frederick Handel
(1685–1759)

Water Music &
Music for the
Royal Fireworks

In a simple arrangement for piano
by Hans-Günter Heumann

English translation
by Julia Rushworth

Drawings by Brigitte Smith

ED 20658

ISMN 979-0-001-16876-2

Mainz · London · Berlin · Madrid · New York · Paris · Prague · Tokyo · Toronto
© 2009 SCHOTT MUSIC GmbH & Co. KG, Mainz · Printed in Germany

Dear Pianists,

In this volume you will find a simple piano arrangement of two popular orchestral works of the Baroque era, *Water Music* and *Music for the Royal Fireworks* by George Frederick Handel (1685–1759). There is an interesting background to the composition of the two works. Three royal barge trips took place along the Thames in London, for which Handel provided the accompaniment of the *Water Music*. The work consists of three suites (compositions consisting of a sequence of several dance movements) with 22 movements altogether. After the end of the War of the Austrian Succession (1741–1748), where the British were among the victors, King George II held a celebration of the peace treaty in London's Green Park in 1749. It was for this occasion that Handel composed his *Music for the Royal Fireworks*, which has six movements and was his second large-scale work for open-air performance, after the *Water Music*.

And now let yourselves be enchanted by Handel's wonderful Baroque sounds.

With best wishes,
Hans-Günter Heumann

Contents

Biography of the Composer George Frederick Handel

1685: born in Halle on the Saale on 23 February. Learned to play the clavichord in secret, because his father, a doctor, thought a career as a musician would be poorly paid, insecure and low in status.

1693: the Duke of Saxe-Weissenfels, pleased with Handel's organ playing, sent him to study with the organist F. W. Zachov

1702: studied Law at the University of Halle and worked as an organist

1703: second violinist in the Hamburg opera orchestra *am Gänsemarkt*; appointed *Maestro al Cembalo* soon afterwards

1705: first major triumphs as an operatic composer

1706: studied and wrote music in Florence, Rome, Naples and Venice

1710: left Italy as one of the most celebrated composers in Europe. Director of music at the Electoral Court in Hanover. Travelled to London.

1712: settled permanently in London

1719: Artistic Director at the Royal Academy of Music (until 1728), with the task of introducing Italian opera to England. Sensationally successful operas; the most celebrated composer of his time.

1727: granted British nationality

1741: turned away from the genre of opera to concentrate on religious oratorios

1753: went completely blind

1759: died in London on 14 April. Buried in the grandeur of Westminster Abbey. He left a considerable fortune.

History of the work: Water Music

There are three suites with 22 movements altogether (HWV 348–350).
The suites were written at various different times. The exact dates of composition cannot be established beyond doubt, as almost all the original manuscript scores (music written out by Handel himself) have been lost. This also makes it impossible to determine the structure or the order of pieces in the suites.

King George I took three royal barge trips on the Thames, for which Handel provided the accompaniment of the *Water Music*:
The first barge trip was on 22 August 1715 from Whitehall to Limehouse. On this trip Handel is said to have been reconciled with the King, his former employer in Hanover. The rift between them had been caused by Handel's departure from Hanover for London.
The second barge trip was on 17 June 1717 from Whitehall to Chelsea and back. On this second trip the King liked the music so much he had it played again twice.
The third barge trip was on 26 April 1736, in the company of Crown Prince Frederick and Princess Augusta of Saxe-Coburg-Gotha.

The instrumentation varies in the three suites:
Suite No. 1 in F major: 2 horns, 2 oboes, bassoon, strings, harpsichord
Suite No. 2 in D major: 2 trumpets, 2 horns, 2 oboes, bassoon, strings, harpsichord
Suite No. 3 in G major: flute, piccolo, strings, harpsichord

Handel and King George I of England on the Thames during a performance of Handel's *Water Music*.

Adagio e staccato

from Suite No. 1 in F major HWV 348, 2nd movement

© 2009 Schott Music GmbH & Co. KG, Mainz

Air*)

from Suite No. 1 in F major HWV 348, 6ᵗʰ movement

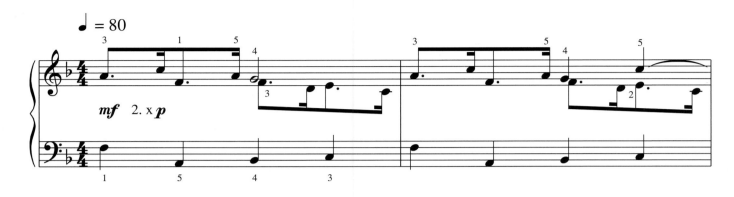

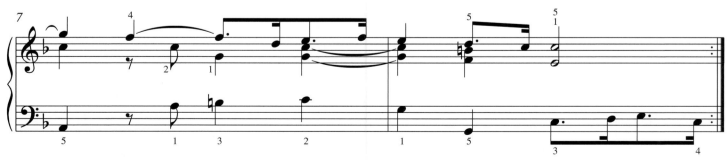

© 2009 Schott Music GmbH & Co. KG, Mainz

*) **Air** (Fr. = melody) was used in the 16ᵗʰ and 17ᵗʰ Centuries for a solo song with lute accompaniment. Later on the name was also used for instrumental pieces with tuneful melodies, which might be included in a suite.

Minuet *)

from Suite No. 1 in F major HWV 348, 7th movement

♩ = 144

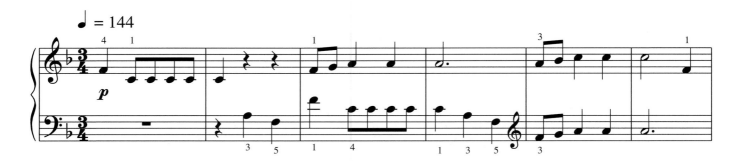

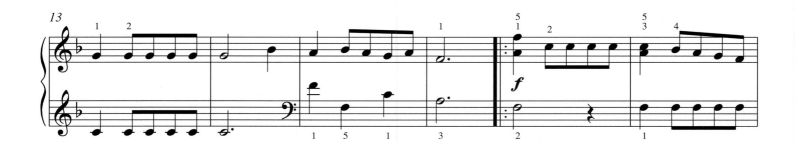

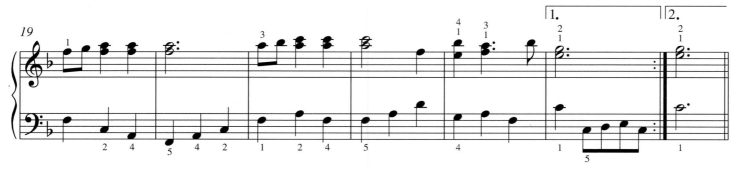

© 2009 Schott Music GmbH & Co. KG, Mainz

*) **Minuet** (Fr.: menuet) was the most popular courtly dance in the 17th and 18th Centuries, developed into the most elegant of dance forms at the court of the Sun King Louis XIV in France. The minuet is a ballroom dance in 3/4 time at moderate speed. It is danced with small steps (fr. *menu pas* = little step) and numerous embellishments and bows.

Trio

Bourrée *)

from Suite No. 1 in F major HWV 348, 8th movement

© 2009 Schott Music GmbH & Co. KG, Mainz

*) The **Bourrée** was originally a French folk dance, danced by farmers or peasants in clogs. In about 1565 it became a court dance and remained popular well into the 18th Century. The lively *Bourrée* is in 2/2 time and begins on an upbeat.

Hornpipe*⁾

from Suite No. 1 in F major HWV 348, 9th movement

© 2009 Schott Music GmbH & Co. KG, Mainz

*) The **Hornpipe** is a traditional polyphonic English, Irish or Scottish dance piece in lively 3/2 time. It is **named after** the ancient Scottish and Irish wind instrument of the same name. It was originally danced wearing clogs.

Alla Hornpipe

from Suite No. 2 in D major HWV 349, 2nd movement

© 2009 Schott Music GmbH & Co. KG, Mainz

Fine

D.C. al Fine

Minuet

from Suite No. 2 in D major HWV 349, 3rd movement

© 2009 Schott Music GmbH & Co. KG, Mainz

Lentement *)

from Suite No. 2 in D major HWV 349, 4th movement

© 2009 Schott Music GmbH & Co. KG, Mainz

*) Fr. = slowly

D.C. al Fine

Minuet

from Suite No. 3 in G major HWV 350,
1st movement

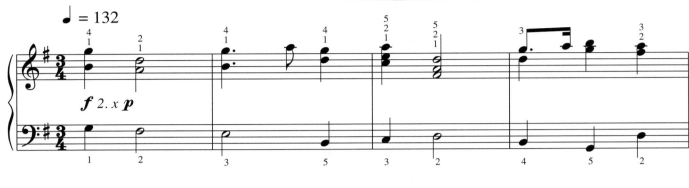

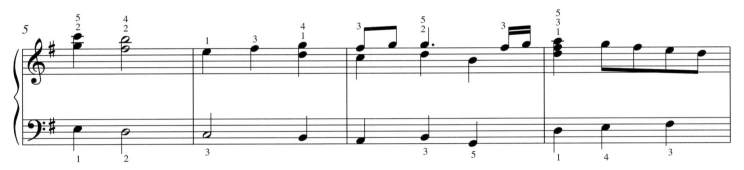

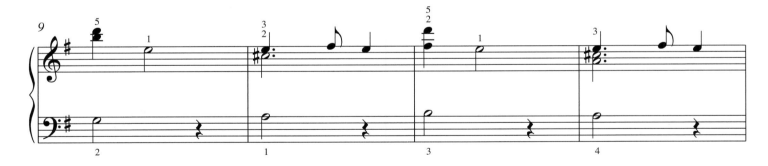

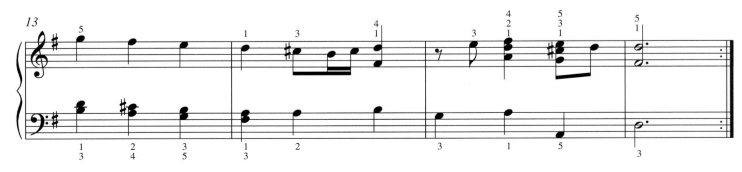

© 2009 Schott Music GmbH & Co. KG, Mainz

Minuet

from Suite No. 3 in G major HWV 350, 4th movement

© 2009 Schott Music GmbH & Co. KG, Mainz

Fine

D.C. al Fine

History of the work:
Music for the Royal Fireworks

Six movements (HWV 351)
Written in March/April 1749
First performed in Green Park, London on 27 April 1749. The fireworks began after the overture (1st movement).
Composed to celebrate the 1748 Treaty of Aix-la-Chapelle, which ended the War of the Austrian Succession. English troops had been involved in the war, so a celebration was planned for London's Green Park in 1749: Handel was commissioned to write an orchestral work for the occasion.
There is a setting for wind instruments (it was the wish of the King that *warlike* instruments should be used, i.e. no strings) and a concert version with wind instruments, strings and basso continuo, which is now the usual instrumentation for the work.

Fireworks and illuminations on the Thames arranged by the Duke of Richmond in Whitehall on 15 May 1749 in the presence of the King.

Bourrée

from *Music for the Royal Fireworks* in D major HWV 351, 2nd movement

© 2009 Schott Music GmbH & Co. KG, Mainz

La Paix*⁾

from *Music for the Royal Fireworks* in D major HWV 351, 3rd movement

Largo alla Siciliana ♩. = 44

p

© 2009 Schott Music GmbH & Co. KG, Mainz

*) Fr. = peace

La Réjouissance*⁾

from *Music for the Royal Fireworks* in D major HWV 351, 4th movement

© 2009 Schott Music GmbH & Co. KG, Mainz

*) Fr. = joy, jollity, cheerful mood

2. x rit.

Minuet I

from *Music for the Royal Fireworks* in D major HWV 351, 5th movement

© 2009 Schott Music GmbH & Co. KG, Mainz

Minuet II

From *Music for the Royal Fireworks* in D major HWV 351, 6th movement

© 2009 Schott Music GmbH & Co. KG, Mainz

Schott Music, Mainz 53 474